Keep Trying, Travis!

WRITTEN BY JoDEE McCONNAUGHHAY

ILLUSTRATED BY STEPHEN CARPENTER

ISBN 0-7847-1705-2

11 10 09 08 07 06   9 8 7 6 5 4 3

PUBLISHING
Bringing The Word to Life

Cincinnati, Ohio

Travis pedaled. His bike took off in a flash. Then it start to wobble, then lean, and then . . .

CRASH!!

"I can't!" Travis cried, getting up off the ground. He threw off his helmet and stomped all around.

"What's the problem?" asked Dad, running out through the door.

"I can't ride my bike!" Travis pouted some more.

"Oh," said Dad, I don't mean all the clutter and clatter. Something far worse than that is the matter."

"Stop saying, 'I can't.' It will not do. With practice and prayer, God can help you. You must remember what the Bible says, 'I can do everything through him who gives me strength.'"

Travis asked, "But why does God care if I ride my bike? What does it matter to him what I like?"

"God loves us and helps us with big things or small. He wants us to trust him with anything at all.

"When you stay overnight at Zach's but miss your home and want to come back, what is it you should say?"

"'I can do everything through him who gives me strength.'"

"Right!" said Dad. "And if the new boy needs a friend, but you're afraid to talk to him. What is it you should think?"

"'I can do everything through him who gives me strength.'"

"Right!" said Dad. "And if you have trouble reading your book, should you close it up quick without taking a look? No! Instead what should you say?"

"'I can do everything through him who gives me strength.'"

"Great! You know, Travis, many things are hard to do. It takes time to learn something new. But you won't have to work alone when you ask for God's help all along."

Travis looked at the bike laying there, and then closed his eyes and said a prayer.

"Lord, help me learn not to give in if something's hard when I begin. I know you'll give me the strength I need, so I will try until I succeed."

Then grabbing his helmet, Travis said with a grin, "With God's help, I can try again and again!"

I can do everything through him
who gives me strength.
—*Philippians 4:13*